Seasoned Citizens:
Preppers and Beginners
Prepare and Fear No Evil

John L. "Poppa" Snider Sr.

Seasoned Citizens: Preppers and Beginners: Prepare and Fear No Evil

Copyright © 2012 by John L. Snider Sr. All rights reserved.
ISBN-13: 978-1496145901
ISBN-10: 1496145909

The author and his family wish to thank Allen Cowan for his assistance with the publication of this book.

For Dae

Introduction

Fear No Evil is about self-confidence and preparedness for citizens fifty or over. It is intended as a guideline to assist and motivate people on the path to self-reliance.

It should be noted and thus highlighted that I am not preparing for the end of the world. Indeed this guide is for making your family self-reliant for any disaster or calamity—by preparing and learning life-sustaining knowledge to see a family through transitory troubled times; to facilitate survival up to four months or until order is restored to your neighborhood. The guide prepares folks to leave their homes, surviving to re-enforce your home long enough for better times to come back.

And, I promise you, they will come back. I know.

My mom, 14 at the time, lived with her parents in Liege, Belgium. One fateful day the Germans invaded her small town. Mom believed those were the never-ending darkest years of her family's life and they were. Mom thought that the world would never recover from the German invasion and the killing machinery of the Third Reich. Her family became resistance fighters, and then paid the ultimate price when the Gestapo arrested Mom, Grandfather and Grandmother.

They were turned in by a priest, of all people.

All three of them were shipped off to separate concentration camps. Grandmother had a harder cross to bear; although Catholic, she was sent to a concentration camp where she was tortured. Mom and her little sister were orphaned and had to fend for themselves. Mom learned much during those dark days and often told me the stories of survival they experienced.

During the last months of 1944, my dad's army unit liberated the concentration camp hours before my grandmother was to be executed, freeing the emaciated prisoners from the iron hold of the SS.

Mom was one of those liberated. My dad was one of the soldiers who made liberation possible. And that's how my father met my mother. They married, and reunited with her parents, came home to the United States and built a wonderful life together. And yet, they understood that the trials and tribulations of life weren't over.

Undeniably, fate would rear its ugly head again, and they always prepared in some way for that day. They didn't know it, but they were "Preppers."

My grandmother, Jeannie Parent, later received the civilian Medal of Honor. She has a place in the Congressional Record of the United States and appropriately her story is next to John F. Kennedy and the heroic sequence of events about PT 109.

The Fear No Evil guide is designed to inspire people into thinking about being independent during a crisis. The guide includes Poppa tips, things that I have learned over nearly forty years from some of the best, not only my elders, but instructors, researchers, experience, and like-minded friends.

My father's family hails from the Ozarks of Missouri, which was a veritable plethora of information for me in my youth. Growing up in New Jersey I had little appreciation for the gifts they were always trying to teach me. It wasn't until my military experience and then moving to North Carolina that I learned the various pieces of my life actually fit into a wonderful life-sustaining puzzle. As my grandfather in North Carolina once told me, "Son, the Carolinas is God's country; good weather most days and good ground that a man can live off and raise a family." He was right; I did that myself and never looked back.

Come with me and we will learn together how to keep ourselves independent during adversity, safe in the knowledge that we can rebuild no matter what our age or circumstance. And always remember, Fear No Evil.

Look around your home.

How much food do you have in the kitchen? What about that meat in the freezer? What happens if the power goes out? Say, how much money is in the house besides the change in the piggy bank? By the way, when's the last time you checked those batteries for the flashlight Aunt Martha gave you last year? Got anything besides birthday candles in the dining room drawer?

After reading Fear No Evil, anyone young or old will have the basics to become self-reliant when misfortune knocks.

There is a fine line between becoming a victim or a survivor. Is your family prepared to live independently from FEMA camps? Our planet is changing rapidly, and weather is becoming unpredictable. The world's global financial position is teetering in a seemingly never-ending balancing act that may topple.

No, it's not the end of the world, but life will be disrupted. While the planet and society reset themselves, folks that are prepared will survive and thrive.

Have you prepared to care for the sick or elderly family members in your home? What about pets? As a new young family or single mom are you self-reliant? Fear No Evil will get you started in achieving those goals and objectives.

Prepare and Fear No Evil

Evil.

It's much like fire. When left uncontrolled it has a mind of its own, feeding on the elements of fuel, oxygen, and heat. As I've always told my family, fire can be and indeed is an uncontrollable monster, ready to gobble up anything in its path when left unsupervised. Even when controlled, fire will rarely be your friend but more of a worthy adversary that requires constant attention.

Fire is a demanding mistress that must be controlled. Once control is removed from the equation, fire will become the ultimate master. Evil is the same way and lessons should be taken from our firefighters, police, bail enforcers, and soldiers, along with any other professions that regularly deal with danger. This guide is about fear—fear that one feels during a catastrophic traumatic event.

Fear, like fire must, be controlled. We must take away the elements that cause fear, exactly like we do with fire. The unknown is fear and when confronted with fear the clinical reaction is fight, flight, or freeze. By preparing for fear and all the baggage it brings, we can at least to some extent control it, thereby, highlighting the Fear No Evil doctrine that those like us live by.

I inadvertently became involved with preparing my family for what is now called the "Sh*t Hit The Fan" scenario which is known by its common acronym SHTF.

It started about 35 years ago. Back in those days we lived through some tough times: limited money; ice storms; power failures and even a hurricane called Hugo that for 30 days left us without power, heat and water.

Always during those trying periods we simply broke out the camping gear and survived the disaster with a minimum of heartache. And because of my hobbies, which involved camping and hunting, no one thought my preparations were unusual. As a police officer I often consulted families on how to prepare "safe rooms." Not for a pending disaster, but mostly for protection against random crimes.

In the late '90s, I realized that I needed to increase my preparedness and I did. Then when my home in a quiet county got annexed into the busy city limits of Charlotte, North Carolina, I understood I would not be able to protect my little empire from the marauding hordes that would take what I had spent so many years to build. Therefore I had to re-evaluate my position. I have done that. I would like to share some of what I've learned over the years with folks of like minds as I learn much from them as well.

Prepping is a fairly easy task for a young family especially with the technology that the Internet brings to the table. But our senior citizens and special-needs citizens have a more difficult challenge. Because of the world changing, and turn of events, these folks are now wondering who will help them when calamity strikes. Many of our senior and special-needs citizens don't have the equipment or skills necessary to negotiate the Internet and therefore need another way to begin basic prepping.

Fear No Evil will help guide the new Preppers with limited resources to handle basic prepping.

If the past teaches us anything it certainly won't be the government stepping up to the plate. So you have to take care of your own and do it properly. I am of the mindset to Fear No Evil, face your problems head on and I want the reader to feel the same way.

There are only two things to do in an SHTF. Scenario—Bug-Out or Bug-In. There are no other options.

You and your family should be prepared for both scenarios. Bugging out is an old military term for, "Let's get the hell outta here fast." Basically, you will have to leave your home with all its familiar comforts that you have built over the years, and literally walk away, to perhaps an unknown safer place. Foregoing all that is right in your life and in some cases the family pets.

This is an emotional decision to make, but we must survive and if leaving the homestead where all the kids grew up and your greatest memories have been built, then so be it.

Survival and re-building must be your primary concern. If you can't deal with that, then stay where you are and die with your memories. It's a personal choice we all must make. Considerations must be made for disabled family members that require constant home care, those with dementia or who need sophisticated machines to keep them alive. Friends, these are all personal choices and I have no right to question your decisions in these matters.

If you decide to Bug Out, here are the guidelines:

1st Poppa tip: Stay away from government camps. They will be filled with thieves, scammers, contagious sick people and other undesirables. Your bug-out bag will help keep you independent from the masses. If you must be around these camps or masses of people always wear an N-95 facial mask to protect against whatever airborne pandemics are present. They can be purchased at your local home improvement store or on the Internet.

Prepping is a long-term, ongoing process that require a lot of planning. Additionally, it must be understood that it's more than a hobby—it's a way of life. In your new environment you'll find the lifestyle rewarding, knowing you are prepared for any situation life throws at you.

Actually, prepping is insurance that is tangible and nearly completely controllable. You can spend as little or as much as your budget allows. Remember, you are preparing for all types of threats, everything from a nuclear power plant explosion, virus pandemic, collapse of the monetary system, and weather disasters to the end of the world as predicted allegedly by the Mayans, if you believe in such a thing. I don't, but then again I didn't believe in the Y-2K finale either.

The last resort is the Bug-out bag, or as I call it, BOB.

The BOB should contain everything one needs for a minimum of 72 hours of being away from home. Preparing a bag to last four weeks is even better. So, step one, have each member of your household go to a sporting-goods store and get fitted with a backpack. Measurement is important here for comfort. The pack will weigh between 30 and 45 pounds when full and must have a minimum of 3,000 cubic inches.

The proper phases of survival are shelter, fire, water and food. Shelter to protect you from the elements, such as a light yet well-built, four-season tent.

Fire to cook with, but more importantly to purify water; and of course, food; not the food from your cabinets. You will need long-term easy packing survival food such as freeze dried or dehydrated bags of camping food. Stock up on them when you can. They are nice to have around the house if the groceries run out. Remember, toasted bread will last twice as long as fresh bread. Cook meat or make long lasting jerky.

If you are working within budget constraints, go to an Army surplus store. It will amaze you what's available for just a few dollars.

Internet sites are best for real deals. Long-term food can be made in your own kitchen in the form of jerky meat and you can dehydrate almost anything . Learn how to make corn dodgers, which are corn meal or wheat cakes that last for months, a popular food of our forefathers. Salted bacon is a fine pack food. Rice and noodles are a good choice for long-term storage as well as pack food. No dehydrator--- just use the oven at low temperatures.

Now, let's look at some other important items to be in the BOB. Are you familiar with what's called flash drives or smart drives, which are key-fob sized computer storage devices? For this project you'll need a computer and a scanner along with the portable flash drive. These drives can be purchased at almost any retail store. Buy one with what they call at least three gigabytes, which is a computer term for the amount of space or data the drive holds.

Scan into the drive the following documents:

Driver license
Social Security card
Marriage license

Medication you take
Medical records
Allergic reactions
Weapons permit
Picture ID
Family documents
Professional licenses
Family photos
Passport

2nd Poppa Tip: Many of our senior citizens don't own a computer. Not to worry; take the above items to your local Wal-Mart and someone there, most likely in the photo department, will prepare the flash drive for you. DO NOT include banking or password information on this drive. Purchase another drive for financial and investment information, which can include account numbers, but not bank routing numbers or passwords. Computer savvy technicians can break or bypass coded devices.

You will need these documents when order is restored to prove who you are for insurance companies, financial institutions, or the government in the event you lose or can't return to your home.

BOB packs are seasonal, and your winter pack with its warm clothes will be heavier than your summer pack. Have a set of durable clothes and boots at the ready and not jeans. Although tough, jeans are really heavy when wet with little insulating value in the winter and they are hot in the summer.

Cabela's has a selection of outdoor seasonal clothes. Order its catalog for seasonal sales. www.campmor.com has great deals as well. Remember to make a pack map that shows in which pockets of the pack your gear is in. It's easy to forget which part of the pack has the small items.

Pack basics, before the food:

Custom built medical pouch
Waterproof matches
Spare lighters
Ferro-magnesium fire stick
Portable cook stove
Camp pots and pans

Flashlight and candles
Cordage (Para-cord)
1 set spare clothes
Month or more of meds
10X10 tarp
Local map
Sleeping bag
2 pair extra socks
Camp shoes (such as Crocs)
Hygiene kit
Toilet paper
Multi-tool
Camp knife
Knife sharpener
Cooking utensils
N-95 surgical face masks
Work gloves
Nalgene or canteens
Emergency Mylar blankets
Compass/GPS
Small shovel

BOBs are personal in nature and this guide is meant merely as an outline of what to pack. I can't tell you what to pack. But I can share with you some items you will need. This BOB must always be packed and ready to go for each family member. Remember, well packed backpacks will keep you and yours independent as you make your way to a safe place—be it kin, friend's property or just a remote area to wait out until order is restored.

3rd Poppa tip: Don't pack your sleeping bag until the last minute as a compressed bag loses its ability to warm you properly. Your bag should be stored in a hanging position.

Down bags are warmer than synthetic materials, but once a down bag gets wet it's useless. Always protect it from moisture or water at all costs.

My gear and pack map

Here is an example of a pack kit map for my summer <u>A</u>ll-purpose
<u>L</u>ightweight <u>I</u>ndividual <u>C</u>arry <u>E</u>quipment. There are more modern
military and civilian packs, but I've carried the large ALICE since
my army days and I've only replaced it twice in nearly 40 years. The
pack is what the kids call "Bullet Proof," meaning it's extremely
durable. Also, old army gear has a tendency to get heavy when wet
unless you have a pack cover, but it works for me and you should
find a backpack that fits your liking.

As you can see by this gear list I'm pretty old school and
there are no frills in my pack. A simple GI canteen and a cooking
system based on burning wood, or burn tabs. My GI mess kit is
normally with me because it makes a great fry pan/steamer.

<u>M</u>odular <u>L</u>ightweight <u>L</u>oad-carrying <u>E</u>quipment is often
compatible with ALICE. I would not use ALICE/MOLLE as a long
distance hiker, but I like it for eight to ten mile trips. That's about as
far as my old back and legs take me these days. Plus, you won't
travel much more than that during a bug-out, as it's a cautious travel.
I do have a small homemade alcohol stove that I can cook on during
rainy downpours. I prefer stainless steel camp pots even though food
sticks to stainless more than other metals. Military gear is aluminum
for the most part.

You can find some items made from stainless steel. Army mess kits appear to be stainless because they are high-grade aluminum. I never use my Teflon pans because the Teflon will chip off into the food. They were retired to the barter bag. (See barter bag section.)

I keep a Tupperware shoebox to store my food in to ensure it stays dry along with a one gallon Ziploc bag which I call my floater bag that holds another two pounds of food and supplements, enough food for six days on the road which I can increase with hunting-fishing when feasible. By cutting the rations in half they'll last twelve days. If I were in a bug-out position I would increase the poundage to 12 that I can extend to 24 days without re-supply.

The food is designed to give me energy-boosting carbohydrates which will be needed especially if one is diabetic, even Type 2, because the calories burned up during a bug out scenario will far outweigh the carbohydrate intake. With the condiments I carry I can make various meals from the noodles or rice. Chicken or beef bouillon cubes are quite good with rice, and very lightweight.

In the top flap of my pack is a 10x12 light-weight Hennessey tarp which I can pull out during a rainstorm without having to look through the whole pack, then I can set up my hammock up to avoid getting wet. The tarp should be kept handy. Have a good chopping knife and a smaller camp knife; keep several if you can as they are an invaluable tool to have. You may notice some items are duplicated, like fire-making tools because I'm just not into rubbing two sticks together. I know how to do it; I really just hate doing it. Some items have weight values next to them because they are equipment concerns for me.

Testing Your BOB

I should have called this exercise, "Dawg, I didn't see that one coming." Well, here you are, you've been working on your BOB for weeks, months even, and you're really proud of yourself; yes sir, I really am prepared now. That's for sure.

NOT!

Now it's time to find a state or national park and spend two or three glorious days and nights in the field. I did this with my best friend a few years ago; it was a real treat. Try to go during the work week if possible as the park will be less crowded.

We parked the Jeep Wrangler, put on our BOBs and headed for the trail. My buddy had just put out his cigarette and was enthusiastic to hit the trail. He donned his much too heavy pack and we headed north.

Just a little bit into the trailhead my wheezing pal asked, "Say, how far you think we've gone so far?"

I stopped and turned around to stare at his sweaty face. "Well my friend, if you turn around you can see the Jeep parked in the lot over there."

He was crushed.

We had a good laugh at his expense. But a valuable lesson was learned—all the preparation looked good on paper and in theory he was truly prepared. However the reality was this was gonna hurt and hurt bad, and it did; he was in suck city. He still refers to that trip as the camp from hell. But he can now pack a kit for sure.

The first experience you'll find when testing is that like my buddy, your pack is probably too heavy. Then as my friend found out, his feet were sore and he was a getting a hot spot on the back of his ankle from the new boots that didn't quite fit properly.

When we were deep into the trail, he lost track of direction under the thick canopy and couldn't tell which way was north. He thought that was okay because he had a super duper Global Positioning Satellite (GPS) system that would guide us home. There were two problems with his GPS. First, it was misreading, as the signal could not penetrate through the thick leafy canopy. Then on day two he had forgotten to turn off the unit when we made camp and that night the batteries died. Now the GPS was dead weight. My military Lensatic compass, on the other hand, was working just fine.

At the end of the first day he was exhausted and as we tried to make camp he couldn't remember which pocket he had packed his various items in. Long story short, I had to leave camp for a while and find a phone booth so I could change into my cape and save the day.

After walking most of the day, that night he took off his boots to wear his more comfortable camp shoes. The next morning his feet were so swollen he couldn't put the boots back on. I had told him to just loosen the laces and leave the boots on, but oh no! What do I know? Oh well! At least I was able to doctor up his blisters with moleskin and duct tape. After soaking his feet in the cold creek water he continued on without complaint. Ah! My personal hero!

The second night we had high winds and heavy rain which subsequently caused much of my friend's cheap, "I-got- a-great-deal" equipment to fail. I, on the other hand, enjoyed a soulful night of rest in my state-of-the-art Hennessey hammock. The high winds simply rocked me to sleep like a baby in momma's arms. The next morning our little camper was tired, dehydrated, constipated and just not feeling like Daniel Boone anymore.

A few weekends later we had a debriefing over a pot of hot coffee. Plainly put, he had packed too much including a camp stool, for goodness' sake, plus a large part of his gear was cheap and not field-worthy.

The gear he did bring was not multi-purpose like a canteen cup, which can be used to drink or cook in. I've used my good ole canteen cup to shave in. In fact, I've used mine even as a shovel to dig a "cat hole." It's a stainless steel Nalgene bottle which I not only carried water in, but was able to purify the creek water in as well, and then later that night boiled noodles in for our dinner. I brought hand sanitizer too, not only for disinfecting our hands, but it can also be used to kill bacteria on the camp knife or poured over a small cloth to start a fire. Always be sure to pack items that have multi-use purposes when available.

Most folks, when packing a BOB, tend to over pack. When I talk to other new Preppers they often want to show me their pack, much like new parents showing off their baby for the first time. The first check I make is to lift the bag and assess its weight. I'll find that more often than not the pack is remarkably heavy. When we weigh the pack on a scale I'll find it weighing in at more than 60 pounds. That's a respectful weight for a young person or a soldier that is fit as a fiddle and able to comfortably carry serious weight, but not for most citizens.

This type of load for a Seasoned Citizen would be a nightmare to carry and certainly shorten the distance one would be able to walk. I prefer the pack weight to be strictly less than 45 pounds. Even this weight will be a burden when walking miles and miles. Packing your bag is a work in progress and the contents of the bag will change with the equipment you have, as well as the seasons.

Keep in mind that your trip food at a minimum of one pound per day will add three to six pounds to your pack. Pack food should be supplemented with fresh food as much as possible. This can be done by foraging and bartering along the way. (Remember the barter bag.) Or, if you have the skills and the equipment needed to hunt or fish. Weight is a constant logistical problem. Just one quart of water weighs 2.5 pounds. Sleeping bags can weigh as little as two pounds to eight pounds, depending on their temperature rating.

New state-of-the-art hammocks are typically lighter than tents and in my humble opinion much more comfortable, you can even sleep on your side. Plus they are self-contained like a tent. My friends love to joke and call them Burritos for bears.

When it comes to packing don't fall into the trap of "Gee! I really don't need this item now, but golly! I may need it later. I better bring it just to be safe." So there is a method to the madness of packing, experiment often until your bag weight is where you want it to be. Keep in mind there is a huge difference in packing durable gear versus cheap gear. For example, a new stainless-steel, dog-food bowl without lead in it is a good dish or soup bowl. It's cheap, yet durable and has multiple uses.

As a general rule when packing and distributing your paraphernalia among a group, plan on losing one third of your food or equipment. Entire packs and all that goes with them can be lost when crossing rivers. Packs can, and if not properly guarded, will be stolen right from under your nose in some cases. Spread the gear out when moving with a group, and don't put all the food or tools in one pack. Delegate it to several individuals then mark it on the leader's pack map so if a pack or bag comes up missing you will be able to tell at a glance what has been lost.

Toddler packs are helpful as the children can carry their toys and snacks. Pack small easy toys and play books. Start preparing them now with small day trips along with some simple home drills as you would when teaching them about fire drills. Dress them in lighter colors to avoid bug bites. Tuck their pants into their socks. Avoid spraying their delicate skin with DEET. Check often for rashes.

ALICE PACK MAPPING SYSTEM
Approximate total ALICE weight: 34 lbs
Estimated field weight 36 lbs
Fully loaded
ALICE EMPTY with the metal frame = 8 lbs
With modifications and added pouches

100   Flap pouch Pocket
        Hennessey Tarp

101   Interior radio pocket
        EMPTY

102   Main pack bay
        Hennessey Hammock 2.25 lbs
        Floater bag
        Sleeping bag
        Poncho Wobbie Liner
        Liter bottle for water purification
        Food locker 4.0 lbs
        BDU blouse 1.5 lbs
        sleeping pad
        Mess kit 1.25 lbs
        Smaller barter bag
        Hygiene kit

Poncho
Mylar emergency blanket
Spare cordage
Hygiene kit 1.75
Toilet paper
Toothbrush
Hand sanitizer
Spare reading glasses
Oral B Brush ups (3)
Small Duct tape
Spray anti-septic
Small Neosporin
Shave cream pouch
Razor
Small brush
Soap box
Benadryl 6 doses
Motrin 4 doses
GI multi use soap
Super glue
Oral floss
Cortisone

103   Tool Kit (Army 30 magazine ammo pouch) 4 lbs loaded
        Pocket fishing kit 8 oz
        Laplander saw (arguably one of the best bush craft saws
        available)
        Multi knife sharpener
        Screw shovel handle for the Coleman
        GPS manual (I do use GPS as a backup)

104   U.S. Army ammo pouch (20 round magazines)
        Bug spray
        LSA oil
        Hand sanitizer
        FOB dry fire cubes

105   Holder strap nylon
        Coleman shovel w/o the handle 1.25 lbs

106   Small left pocket
        Main funding items and the flash computer drives

107   Small center pocket
        Work gloves and surgical rubber gloves also the
        STRIKEFORCE w/dry fire cubes

108   Small right pocket
        Perlite cigar stove w/ranger bands (2)
        2 bottles of denatured alcohol total 6 or 7 oz
        Black BIC lighter
        Waterproof matches
        Additional Bic types (small)

109   Large left pocket
        Trangia cook pot rectangular (Swedish product, see the
        review)
        Emergency AW-600
        Scrub pad
        Camp soap
        Cotton balls
        Ferro rod mini
        Waterproof matches
        Tea candle
        Chow set knife, fork, and spoon.

110   Large center pocket
        Spare heavy socks
        Spare light socks
        Camouflage bandana
        Army helmet soft hat (cloth hat I use when sleeping for heat
        control)
        Spare camouflage dew-rag
        Mirror (important when inspecting private areas) for shaving,
        signaling, etc.

111   Large right pocket
        Cordage paracord and 2 100-foot roles of jute twine
        Bug head net (can be used for fishing)

Lightweight stakes for the tarp and hammock (can be used
for digging)

112   LBE strap: acronym for Load Bearing Equipment (pack
         straps)
         GPS system (I do use GPS as a backup for my compass)

113   Holster strap nylon (left)
         HK-USP 45 caliber pistol or the Storm 9 MM pistol

114   GI canteen holder
         Canteen, canteen stove, canteen cup and a hard cover for the
         cup when cooking

4th Poppa tip: The stainless steel hard coverlid for my canteen cup
is the same kidney shape as the cup. It was designed exactly for the
GI canteen cup. There is also a rubber lid that is very handy with a
sip port built in. These items can be found at
www.canteenshop.com., a small company run by Rob Simpson and
who stocks the hard to find items at great prices. The best part is he
is a self-reliant practitioner himself. Never ever buy Chinese made
GI equipment, not only are the products poorly made they are also
produced in varying sizes making the different components that are
supposed to work together in the field useless.

Chow locker:

         Dehydrated noodle shells
         10 oz Bannock
         Cheese powder
         Butter powder
         Onion powder
         Dry rice
         Country gravy
         Honey (2) packs
         Sugar
         60 corn dodgers
         Rice-A-Roni Cheese
         Pouring funnel
         MRE cheese (2)

MRE PB&J (2)
My own jerky

Float Bag:

Mountain House meals (3)
Spice bag
Raisins
X-salt & pepper
Tea bags (3)
Bouillon (2)
Olive oil (3)
Coffee bags (3)
Parmesan cheese

5th Poppa tip: These small packets of food can be purchased at www.minimus.com, which is a company that specializes in stocking small travel size portions of food and personal items. TSA approved items are available.

Maxpedition 10X4 Water carrier purification kit:

Maxpedition makes some of the finest bags/packs in the world. They can be a bit pricey, but worth their weight in gold when in the bush. Extremely durable and reliable.

Ferro rod
LED light
Survival whistle
Guyut steel bottle
Lexan MRE spoon
GSI drink / cook cup
Frontier Pro water filter
Poison ivy spray
P-38 can opener (army)
V-Cotton fire balls
GIS cup handles
Heat sock
Extra coffee bags
Aquamira tabs pack

D Ring non-climb
Iodine tabs
Vitamin C tabs (water), kills the iodine taste
Spare Frontier filters
8% DEET

6th Poppa tip: Coat cotton balls with Vaseline and store in a plastic bag. They are excellent fire starters that will ignite with just a spark and burn hot for several minutes. Excellent for starting wet tinder. Lint from a dryer makes a marvelous fire starter, plus it's free.

Sanitation – field

Friends, I can't express how important sanitation is in an SHTF
scenario. It's not something we normally talk about in this country
because we are trained from our earliest years on how to keep
ourselves clean. Well, at least the majority of us are. Frankly it's a
distasteful topic to discuss. However it is certainly a topic that must
be addressed.

Today it seems like every morning when I turn on the news
another food product has been tainted by salmonella, or some other
nasty waste-causing virus. We all know how utterly filthy a public
restroom can be. Let's face the facts, not all our friends and
neighbors are the cleanest folks on the planet. Man in the form of
poor farm-waste management also creates animal waste that causes
illness we often experience in food.

Sanitation at home during a situation is difficult but
manageable. Personal sanitation in a bug-out scenario is just plain
difficult for most folks, but if you follow the subsequent guidelines
you can make the chore more comfortable.

The bad news is human waste is nasty. The good
news…Hey! It's biodegradable, so when properly disposed of it's no
longer a problem.

When bugging out we'll use what the campers call "cat holes." I carry a small steel Coleman folding shovel with a built-in pick to dig the cat hole, which I make about six to ten inches deep. Many outdoor types carry a lightweight plastic trowel; they are real prone to breaking at the worst times. My steel Coleman is a multi-purpose tool that can dig through even the toughest earth. It seems like without fail while I'm doing my business, flies and large, ugly horseflies swarm my cat hole. (Especially in the spring,)

These bugs (pun intended) will be a pain in your ass! To remedy this assault on your position carry a few shovels of campfire ash and cover your little guys before washing yourself, then add another scoop to cover the material you cleansed with. This should keep the invaders at bay.

Once your task is complete cover the cat hole with dirt and then use the surrounding indigenous leaves and twigs to cover the dig hole. Complete the mini-adventure by placing a large rock on top of the former hole, forever entombing the little guys and protecting them from coyotes, raccoons and such that will try as best they can to grave-rob your site, spreading disease and pestilence among your fellow Preppers. The other benefit: no one will know you were ever there. Remember, when voiding in the field stay away from any form of water.

Another powerful point to keep in mind is the material you use to clean yourself. I mean you can only carry so much toilet paper. Once out of this luxurious item you'll be forced to use the local foliage.

This can cause what I tell my grandchildren is "monkey butt," a very uncomfortable itchy feeling of being unclean. When I run out of toilet paper on long trips I will use a piece of cloth for cleansing, then vigorously wash the cloth so it can be re-used. Occasionally I will boil the rag to ensure it is bacteria-free. Diapers must be washed and boiled each night.

Keep your hands clean and away from your face until they are sanitary. Fingernails should not be overlooked, as they will get grimy when doing camp chores. Keep your hairs short including the pubic area as our groins are Club-Med for lice, chiggers and ticks.

Only drink from your cup or your canteen even with the grandchildren. Friends, the spread of disease in the group can be avoided by simply not sharing cups or utensils. Most all tree branches have bacteria growing under the bark so before putting that meat on your stick, skin the bark back and hold the stick over the fire for a minute. Biodegradable camp soap and hand sanitizers are you friends when bugging out.

7th Poppa tip: Soap will not lather up in seawater no matter how hard you try. If you run out of soap use some charcoal from the cook fire with just a bit of ash. Ash is lye and it will burn you if you use too much.

In addition to a hat is what's called a "dew-rag," which is a handkerchief or bandana tied over the head covering the hair. It's great for keeping ticks off our heads. In the summer heat, make a wet bandana and tie it around your neck. Keeping the carotid arteries cool is a secret of our forefathers. Watch any old cowboy movie and they all have bandanas around their necks to capture sweat, then let it evaporate, cooling the neck arteries. It wasn't a fashion statement. They were preventing heat stroke and it really works.

Always tuck your pant legs into your boots or inside the socks; keep your belt tight and use DEET spray to deter ticks as well as chiggers. All my life I heard many an old wives' tale about a cure for chigger bites but never found one that worked.

Yep, you just have to wait them out, once they plant their insidious little eggs under your skin they leave like rats deserting a ship. Then the festering begins almost as bad as poison ivy. By the way, in the winter you'll see hairy-type vines going up trees; normally this is dormant poison ivy. Stay well away from it.

If you think you have come in contact with the evil shiny leaf or vine, STOP IMMEDIATELY! Wash and rinse with soap and water. Dry in direct sunlight. Wash any clothing that may have come in contact with ivy or sumac. Then liberally apply a heavy coating of poison ivy relief spray, which comes in pen-sized vials made by StingEze. Staying healthy while moving is imperative. This is not the time to say "Oh! I'll be okay."

Finally, every day or night before sleeping take a damp cloth with some soap if you have it, and rub down your body starting at the head and ending at the feet. Use a clean canteen of water to rinse. Baking powder rubbed briskly into the hair will remove all the oils and sweat that built up from the day's work.

Brushing your teeth and gums frequently is important. When you run out of tooth paste, use a bit of baking soda stash or salt. If you have nothing, take a fresh twig, skin the bark and bite the tip until it spreads out like a mini broom then start brushing your teeth with it. You can also just rub your teeth and gums with a clean finger. Rinse often and always try to keep the mouth moist especially when wearing dentures while sleeping.

Small children will require more attention and keeping them and their clothes clean can be a challenge as can managing additional clothes and cleaning supplies. Washing children as described every day or night is paramount when moving to a safe place.

8th Poppa tip: A small sharp knife makes a very good finger and toenail cutter. Just let your nails grow a bit longer than normal before trimming.

The bug-out vehicle

This section is for urbanites and suburbanites. Folks in rural areas
won't need to spend a lot of time on this subject. Our rural neighbors
in the northern states normally keep a prep bag in their cars loaded
with enough tools, blankets, heat sources, emergency food, etc. Of
course those in desert areas are prone to have the same things but
more storable water for obvious reasons. Plus, the reality is that
many of these folks have four-wheel drive vehicles to get them
around on a daily basis.

A seasoned prepper in the city may own a Cadillac, SUV, or
a new Prepper perhaps a KIA or some such vehicle normally used in
this urban environment. Some of us own special vehicles for our
handicapped members. Well! More than likely these city cars won't
take you cross country when in crises, but they will take you closer
to where you need to be when bugging out, as long as the roads
aren't too clogged with other citizens who are leaving the highly
populated areas and heading for a safer location during a situation.

A bug-out vehicle can be as simple or as sophisticated as you plan it to be. A four-wheel drive pickup truck is a great choice for a bug-out vehicle. Because of my outdoor lifestyle I own a Jeep Wrangler, which is a small, yet durable four-wheel drive vehicle. I rarely wash the little puddle jumper, I never wax it and the vinyl top looks worn-out. It's a sleeper. I can leave it on the roadside for short periods and people will think it's a junker. The engine however is pristine and well maintained. It's all about keeping a low profile.

A Jeep is small and can't carry a whole lot of gear, but it will carry my family's bug-out equipment. We aren't moving, we're bugging-out for a while hopefully to return to our home sooner rather than later. I did see a Jeep some time back with a cute bumper sign that read: Don't follow me, you can't go where I go.

Use caution when traveling by motor vehicle. During a disaster situation if the governments are still intact or martial law has been implemented and soldiers are patrolling, you will be stopped and more often than not, you and your car will be searched. As we have seen during other crises such as hurricane Katrina, the government's answer to looting, crime and panic is to confiscate weapons when and where they find them. Not only from criminals, but also regular citizens who were merely trying to protect and/or defend themselves. When martial law is imposed, your Constitutional rights go out the window. It may be smarter to hike out using these guidelines.

I know that in today's depressed economy with the incredible gas prices we pay, it's hard to keep the gas tank full. Please try to keep your chariot fueled and serviced at all times, ready to go when called upon for duty.

Our country is designed for commuting, unlike Europe where rail along with other means of mass transport is the norm. Europeans buy their fuel by the liter instead of the gallon, basically because of the continent's design. We on the other hand work in the cities then commute home to the suburbs. It's not unusual for a family to drive seven or twenty miles just to eat at a certain restaurant or shop at a mall. The United States depends on vehicular travel to survive. A flaw no doubt we allowed when planning the country's layout with the initiation of interstate highways.

Okay, let's get to the meat here. Your car, like you, should have its own BOB, normally in the form of a box, perhaps a trunk. Some of my friends keep backpacks so they can pick up and walk away. I think this is a very good approach for a vehicle bug-out storage system. I live two miles from my office, which will put me home in 25 minutes.

We should all have some tools in our cars for minor road repairs. The magical duct tape can be used for busted water hose repairs, tears in roofing fabric, to fix a hanging muffler pipe, along with many other maladies that may come your way while being mobile. Keep a roll handy in the house and the car. Road flares are great for nighttime break downs Additionally they're grand for starting wet camp fires as well as lighting dark places.

Make a mini BOB from the items listed in the BOB section; remember, cars get extremely hot in the summer then unbearably cold in the winter. Ensure each season that you rotate out any food or water stored. Never pack anything that you can't afford to lose, like a weapon or valuables. Vehicles are very easy for bad people to break into. So be prepared to lose then replace this equipment, packing accordingly.

The Mylar space blankets and Mylar mummy bags are important to pack. They are inexpensive and small, about the size of an Altoids can.

The down side of these inexpensive Mylar bags is that they are noisy, they tear easily, they are not really reusable and they form condensation during the sleeping period. However, they will keep you warm and they also make wonderful campfire reflectors when a safe campfire is applicable.

A better choice if your budget allows is the SOL thermal sleeping bag distributed by Adventure Medical Kits for about $50, made from a breathable material that retards condensation, is much less noisy and resistant to tears, is warmer and reusable. Real wool blankets are great for a bug-out vehicle. As mentioned, wool retains its warming value even when wet. Fabric treatments in the washing machine make the wool blanket softer. The wool blanket is heavy to pack for most weight-conscious folks; nevertheless, invaluable in a home or vehicle preparations situations.

Every Day Carry: EDC

Absolutely, each time I leave my home I'll have what is called an EDC or Every Day Carry. For example, on my key chain I have a small LED key-fob flashlight that comes in handy so I don't fumble around in the dark. I also have a four-inch folding Gerber pocket-knife. A knife is a valuable tool to have at all times assisting with a multitude of tasks that I face every day, from opening a letter to peeling my lunch apple. Oh yeah! It makes a sweet self-defense weapon in some cases.

Remember, never bring a knife into a government building that has metal scanners. The blade will be confiscated, and worse, you could be arrested for carrying a weapon. Even with a concealed weapon permit, the same holds true for when going to the airport. CCW does not cover knives.

Because my job requires I carry a pistol, I purchased a DRAGO hip pouch that is strapped to my waist and tied down to my leg. It's very similar to the fanny packs that were popular a few years back.

Of course there is a compartment for my weapon and spare magazines. However there is a bay pocket for other items like my credentials along with my wallet. It is a rare occasion for me to carry a wallet in my pants pocket. The bag keeps pickpockets at bay. A technique often applied by these thieves is to take a knife and cut the strap of a bag right off the shoulder. The DRAGO defeats this modus operandi because the sturdy bag is also cinched to my thigh and the DRAGO is small and compact.

There are pockets for my Leatherman multi-tool in addition to my cellular phone. More importantly, I also can carry a gift the kids gave me for Christmas: a Lifeline Survival box. A see-through plastic waterproof box slightly larger than a pack of cigarettes filled with survival type items most of which I sent to the barter box. I refilled the small container with items that are better suited for me in the event of a crisis and will help me get home. Really, that's the purpose for having an EDC kit, there are no luxury items, but your EDC will help you survive until you can get home.

Lifeline survival box
Waterproof box
Container (green) can be used for drinking
Waterproof matches
Toothpicks, plastic
Flashlight and battery
Swiss Army Knife (small)
Whistle red
Folded plastic bag to be used to gather water
Swatch of tin foil
Water tab purifiers (2)
Band-Aids (2)
Multi-tool (small)
P-38 can opener
Medical: burn cream, aspirin, antibiotic cream

You can also use another fantastic product for making this kit. And that is a solidly-built Pelican box that comes in various sizes. It's waterproof and floats. They are expensive but definitely worth every penny. Keeping and maintaining an EDC kit is very important and should be tailored to your particular needs; really, it can be a life saver.

Family pets

Our pets are like family; hell, they are family for most of us. When bugging in, elderly, ill, handicapped family members and pets are not a real concern, because we plan for and around them. The bug out scenario is absolutely a different matter. When traveling the highways and by-ways of our bug-out routes, certain pets will be a problem, such as especially noisy pets like birds or certain dogs that bark whenever they get the urge. Animals of this nature will give away a camp position in mere seconds, thus compromising the entire family's location and safety. A family decision will have to be made prior to a bug out.

Some pets are an asset, like disciplined dogs that can defend the family or at least alert when an intruder is detected. Many of your larger pets can be saddled with saddlebags or panniers, with which they would be able to carry food, meds and water. Goats are a wonderful choice as they can carry a good deal of weight. You don't need to pack their food because they will eat on the trail, actually they will eat the trail. They are friendly, easy to work with, they can produce milk and Lord forbid, a goat is an excellent food source if it becomes necessary. Goats are naturally afraid of water, however, and will stall when crossing even small streams.

Recipes for the bug-out - Don't cook where you sleep

We enjoy eating prepared meals like Mountain House dehydrated camping chow. The meal is a high quality, easy to prepare, cost-effective food. When I was in the army in the field we ate what was called C-Rations. A self-contained meal with everything in it, that even came with a pack of cigarettes, if they were real old.

In today's military they eat what's called the MRE or Meals Ready to Eat. I often hear young soldiers complain about them, but then again that's part of their job to complain. Me, I think MREs are marvelous, but then again I came up with C-Rations and I really complained about them as well. Except when I was voraciously hungry. Then they were delicious.

When my son was a little boy camping with his Pop, he loved getting an MRE. To him it was like opening a big plastic bag full of goodies. "Oh! Wow. Pop, look, M&M candies," or "Pop, I got lemon pound cake."

Yeah, good times and to this day he still enjoys an MRE when in the field. Camp food is also a large part of our home inventory; this food must be rotated every few years. "Hey honey, what's for dinner?"

The MRE is again a self-contained meal with the entrée, snack, powdered drink, coffee and of course dessert. Like the C-Rations they have candy and toiletries even a chemical heater to warm up the meal. Now, ain't that something, a heater. Wow! These meals will keep for years under the proper temperature. Take note, eat no more than two a day; an MRE will constipate you so drink lots of water when eating one. They make civilian MRE foods nearly like the military ones (without heaters). A great company that sells these products is Emergency Essentials. It can be found on the Internet at: www.BePrepared.com. Good folks to deal with.

These days I prefer eating homemade food; my wife makes the best beef jerky you can slip in your mouth. Plus, with my homemade food I can pack more of it and make literally dozens of food combinations, especially if supplemented with a fish or a critter one might catch if the opportunity arises. So I have included a list of recipes that store and carry well. Our forefathers, including the Lewis and Clark expedition, used many of these recipes.

9th Poppa tip: After preparing any dehydrated food at home from meat, gravies, or fruit let the food sit for a day. Then place the bagged food in the freezer for two weeks; this will make them last longer, as well as making them mold resistant. I've been doing this for more than 10 years and have never had food go bad. Critters: country critters taste much better than city critters and have fewer toxins.

Some of my favorites:

Bacon, salt sugar cured: pro-diabetic

Can be purchased online for $29 for about three pounds; the bacon will last for months in the bush. Some may become moldy but mold can be washed off with water and a brush or even cut out. Vinegar will also remove the mold from the meat. While frying the bacon a biscuit of bannock or pieces of hard-tack can be fried in the grease after the meat cooks. The bacon can also be purchased at most grocery stores near the country ham area. It's salty so you may want to soak it in a pan of water first.

Bannock

1 cup of wheat flour, add about one teaspoon or less of baking soda
and a pinch of salt. Kick it up a notch by adding 1 tablespoon of
sugar (brown is real good) and 2 tablespoons of powdered milk. In
the field it's best to place the dry ingredients into a sandwich bag.
When you are ready to cook simply add in a little water and lightly
knead the mixture in the bag until firm. Bannock doesn't like to be
handled too much so little kneading is necessary; it will rise some
after standing for 20 minutes. Serves one

Bannock and country gravy: make in the field

1 cup of mixed bannock
½ cup country gravy
1 cup "gravel" or SPAM
½ cup of water

Mix the bannock with just a small amount of water. Cook the
bannock into a biscuit. Bring 1/2 cup or 4 ounces of water to a boil
then add ½ cup of country gravy. Bring this mixture to a boil then
simmer until the gravy thickens. Prepare the meat; once that is
completed break up the bannock then pour the gravy over the bread
and add the meat. Serves one

Beef Jerky: pro-diabetic, to be prepared at home

7 Pounds London broil, chuck or shoulder roast

Marinade:

One hefty tablespoon:
Liquid Smoke
Vinegar
Teriyaki sauce
Garlic teriyaki
Soy sauce
Brown sugar (Leave out for diabetics)
Tabasco sauce
Worcestershire

Honey
Raw chopped garlic

Dry Rub:

Black pepper
Cracked pepper
Sea salt
Paprika
Garlic powder
Red pepper
Onion powder
Layer the meat and rub in a large Tupperware container overnight.
Place the meat in a tray and paint the marinade on. Dehydrate
halfway, then paint with pure honey. After a few hours turn over and
paint with honey again. Cook time: medium-low heat 10 hours.

Corn dodgers: to be prepared at home

2 cups corn meal
2 TBL Butter
½ TSP Salt
1 TBL Sugar or raw bamboo sugar (milder)
2 cups of milk
1 TSP Baking soda

Pre-heat the oven to 400. Cook the corn meal in a saucepan with
butter, salt, sugar and milk.
Bring to a boil then remove from the heat. Cover the pan and let the
mixture stand for 5 minutes.
Stir in the baking soda and spoon TBL size balls onto a greased
cookie sheet. Bake 10 to 15 minutes until golden brown.

Gravel: to be prepared at home

Take two pounds of lean ground beef and fry in a cast-iron fry pan until well done. Season with salt, pepper, onion powder and garlic. Place the mixture in a dehydrator on low heat for 8 to 10 hours. The mixture will become hard like bits of gravel when done. The gravel can be reconstituted in water for any recipe requiring beef, buffalo or deer. (Very good in spaghetti.) Do not re-hydrate in any type of sauce or gravy, it just doesn't work for some reason. I have kept gravel for well over three years, it's very durable. There is no fat in this meat, which is why you should use it in combination meals. Just feels good knowing there is meat in the pasta.

Hardtack, modified: A good food used during the Civil War. Really hard on the teeth; soften it in coffee or grease before eating. It can also be pounded into flour.

2 cups water
3 TBL of oil
3 TSP salt
1 TBL honey
2 eggs
1 cup powdered milk
1-1/2 cups wheat flour

Knead the mixture then add 4 cups wheat flour slowly until the mixture is very stiff, roll into 4 inch squares, pierce with a fork. Bake at 350 for 15 to 20 minutes.

Parched corn

Dehydrate corn kernels then roast the corn in a slightly oiled fry pan until the corn is a golden brown but not enough to pop. While warm, season with salt, red pepper and garlic powder; it will last for weeks or longer.

Pemmican: pro-diabetic

Pound together or grind ½ pound each of the following:

Jerked meat
Parched corn
Dried cranberries
Dried apples

Bind with vegetable oil (small spoons) and bacon grease.

Mashed potatoes & gravy:

1 cup water with optional chicken bouillon broth
Powdered potatoes
Powdered butter
Powdered milk
Salt & pepper

Meat: Gravel, SPAM or jerky

Heat the water to a boil then add potatoes, butter, milk powder, salt
and pepper. Remove from heat and make sure the mix remains stiff
as when the gravy is added it will loosen. Add the meat and mix and
eat.

Spaghetti

Take 1 heaping tablespoon of tomato soup base, add 1 or 2 cups of
water, stir in one heaping tablespoon of McCormick's spaghetti
seasoning, and stir. Re-hydrate 2 oz of gravel then add to mix. Add
in some raw sugar, garlic powder, salt and pepper with about an
ounce of olive oil, stir in some onion powder mix or better yet a real
onion if you have one. Break up 4 oz of noodles and boil until soft,
add to the tomato gravy, stir and enjoy. You can substitute SPAM
for the gravel.

Prepare at home:

1 tablespoon of tomato base
1 tablespoon of McCormick's spice
1 tablespoon of Italian seasoning
1 tablespoon of raw sugar (bamboo)

The Trangia Aluminum Pan

This product is built in Sweden, the package has an address of Box 5 830 47 Trangsviken, Sweden. It is a rectangular small pan made from high-quality aluminum with a handle that is rubber coated and can be removed from the pan itself. Or the handle can be folded over the pan much like an old Army mess kit. The lid for the pan is milled to such specific standards that when completely closed it seems to be air tight. Cost: $10 to $15 depending on the store.

The pan will hold right at three cups of water or 24 ounces. After boiling the three cups simply add another cup, then one can merely boil one quart of water within a few minutes, depending on the source flame. The pan's dimensions are: 6.5 X 3.5 X 2.6.

I decided to give this pan a shot as it seemed well suited for field duty. Now I expected this item to be very small based on the dimensions I read on the web page, however, I must have mentally misjudged the size of the kit because when the product arrived I found the pan to be actually bigger than I had expected.

I bought this product for my Every Day Carry (Winter EDC) kit that I keep in my Maxpedition JUMBO. In this bag I carry a space-emergency blanket along with a space-emergency sleeping bag, for emergency shelter. Of course the kit has the capability to make fire, process water, and there is a weapon for food procurement or protection. The kit is designed to get me home in my local urban environment.

The Trangia nests nicely in the bottom of the bag and is a multi-use product. The lid for the pan can be used as a dish or cutting board and the Trangia can be easily used with a campfire or a camp burner. The unit has a great deal of storage capacity and because of its tight-fitting lid the objects stored inside are water resistant. The inside of the lid can be polished to the point that the Trangia can be used as a signal mirror. The aluminum is thick enough that the pan could even be used as an emergency shovel.

When filled with three cups of water the pan sits nicely on my "Pocket Rocket" stove. I've used civilian aluminum pots quite a bit over the years and I found when boiling water there would always be a suspicious film or slime in the water, which is why I stopped using a lot of them. The Trangia is made from quality strong aluminum. My first water boiled clean and untainted by any sort of film or glaze.

I am very happy with this product and plan to buy another one for my ALICE pack; it's just a good durable quality piece of equipment.

Without Rule of Law: WROL

Not intended to scare anyone here, but some bad situations could cause us to be in a scenario that is now called "Without-Rule-Of-Law" or WROL. Don't you just love acronyms? If something was to happen so bad that our local governments no longer provide us basic police and fire services we will all be in the popular Hurt Locker. If FEMA along with our emergency civil service were to crumble, we would really be up the proverbial creek without a stout paddle, right?

Maybe, then again maybe not! It's just my humble opinion or perhaps I have more faith in the human race than I should have.

I just seriously doubt things would ever get that bad, at least not exclusive of some type of early warning event. However my personality dictates the wise adage, "Better to have it and not need it, than to need it and not have it." Or prepare for the worst and hope for the best.

Movement

10th Poppa tip: When bugging out it's best to cook and move at night and sleep during the morning hours when the day is still cool. Avoid cooking strong smelling foods like bacon when in a sensitive position as the scent can literally travel for miles. This will alert others to your presence and as a result they will try to liberate your provisions.

Moving at night isn't foolproof, as many citizens have night vision goggles that work on starlight or infrared. Hunters use FLIR devices to locate animals by their heat signature. Covering yourself with a poncho or tarp will lower your heat signature to nearly zero, but it only works for a precious few minutes.

Especially in the beginning of an event, while traveling you must try and stay off the main roads. Additionally, in keeping with staying off the roads you should try to keep your distance from homes that will be watching for trespassers. Remember, most of the people will be trying to protect their property as well, more than likely they'll be on severe high alert, particularly if the rule of law has broken down.

Being more visible during the daylight and moving during these hours is suicide. Never walk out in the open -- as they say in the military, you will become a casualty. Keep your silhouette profile low.

At night stay close to tree lines and never walk too near buildings, empty or not, even if that means taking a detour. Patience is the key when traveling during a bug-out. If you must travel in open areas or desert environments try to stay low and take advantage of creeks, gullies and ravines. No flashlights; they not only give away your position, a light will ruin your night vision. If you must use a light to check a map heading then use a red lens LED light while under a coat, poncho or rain jacket. Night vision will stay intact.

11th Poppa tip: Barking dogs large or small are a threat to your presence. If you can spare the food make small bread and peanut butter balls. An untrained dog will eat these like candy and the sticky peanut butter will shut them up long enough for you to get out of the area. It's an old trick we used when busting drug dealers as we began entry into their fortified homes. Plus, if not needed then you can eat the leftovers.

Keep a low profile when traveling among the public highways and by-ways. Don't draw attention to yourself or your party. Keep as much of your gear concealed as you possibly can, especially weapons. The trick is keeping them out of sight yet accessible. Security is paramount when moving your family at any time, including stormy weather. Never walk too close to each other. It's a natural instinct to stay close to one another when in perilous situations, nevertheless for a hostile defender or shooter it's an easy group target. Make a conscious effort to provide points as well as rear security people when possible.

Establish hand signals. For example, if your point person comes upon an individual or group deemed hostile you should have a pre-determined signal to convey stop, run and hide or start shooting, we are being robbed. My family knows if I remove my hat/bandana it means run and hide. If I remove my headgear then throw it down, it means start shooting, we're in trouble.

We all pack a spare set of clothes when hiking or camping. Many of my friends wear woodland type clothes when in the field because first and foremost they are weather friendly, durable and one can travel unseen when hunting or photographing wildlife. When conducting a movement exercise during hunting seasons, wear bright orange vests.

But they also pack as their spare set, what they call "city clothes," which they use to go into town and re-supply or eat a meal at a restaurant to blend in with the locals. This became popular with the hikers that travel the Appalachian Trail, which if followed all the way through can take a year or more to traverse. The long distance hikers needed to re-supply in the towns along the way and thought it best not to bring too much attention to themselves, again keeping that low profile image.

12th Poppa tip: Instead of folding your spare clothes try rolling them up really tight and putting them in a waterproof plastic bag. They will be wrinkle free and you can use the bag for other things, like collecting water or soaking gamy meat or fish. Even washing your clothes -- a large baggie can be filled with soap and water. Just put the dirty clothes inside, and then tie the bag loosely to your pack. The walking motion will agitate the clothes clean. Then re-fill the bag with fresh clear water to rinse. Great for cloth diapers as well.

In my younger days I would build cache (bazooka) tubes made from PVC pipe. Going to the local home improvement store I would have them cut into six- or eight-inch diameter tubes in two-foot or four-foot lengths then have a screw cap on each end. I would paint them green and fill them with items I didn't or couldn't carry, such as extra food, clothes, fishing kit, spare water, batteries, toilet paper, camera, film or ammunition. I would separate the various items with heavy cardboard circles that I cut to fit the tube's diameter. Before sealing the tubes I would put Teflon tape on the threads prior to placing the caps on to prevent water from seeping in.

In those days, at least once a season, I would try a long-distance hike to test my gear and myself. So months before the trek I would make weekend trips and bury the tubes in strategic locations just below the frost line, almost two feet deep. Over the years we planted more than thirty of these cache tubes; seven are still out there and one, err… got kinda misplaced…. Well, lost, actually; it had to do with some expensive brandy and an unreadable map, but what a great time capsule it'll make. You can buy pre-made bazooka tubes for nearly $200 each or make your own like I did for less than $20.

You can build and place the bazooka tubes along the path for your bug-out location. We have a friend that buries his in cemeteries along the way. The boy is just a tad eccentric, if you know what I mean.

13th Poppa tip: When traveling to your safe zone never, and I mean never, stay in the same camp location more than one night. You must stay on the move and Leave No Trace where you have been. Cook fires should be small, no bigger than a coffee can in circumference, lit only at night to help hide the rising smoke. Thick tree foliage will trap and hold smoke until it slowly dissipates.

House or Apartment dwellers

This deals mostly with the last resort of bugging out. Just for starters I will address bugging-in. I have prepared a list of what one must basically have in your home. Once you have acquired the basics you can now build from this point.

Batteries: at least 20 for each device they are used for
Storm lanterns and several gallons of oil
Hand cranked solar powered radio
Non-battery operated telephone
N-95 surgical masks for pandemic disease
Five gallon buckets with lids
Flashlights
Weapon and ammo
Water and water filter purifiers
Wool blankets that retain their insulating value even when wet

Water: You can buy a "water BOB," which is a food-grade large plastic bag that fits in any standard bathtub. It will hold 100 gallons of water that you fill from the tub faucet and it comes with a hand pump to remove the water into containers. In the event of a pending storm you'll have plenty of time to fill the heavy-duty bag before the power goes out. The cost is less than $40. We bought ours at a company called Cheaper Than Dirt. www.cheaperthandirt.com.

Standard water coolers that can be purchased at your local home improvement store will continue to work even after a power failure, as they are gravity based. The clean water can be bought in five gallon plastic bottles.

With regards to how much water you will need the minimum standard is one gallon per person per day. You'll need one half gallon for drinking, one quart for cooking, and one quart for hygiene.

14th Poppa tip: You can buy emergency packs of drinking water that will last for years. When you tear open a bag or a can of packaged drinking water you'll find the taste offensive; actually it will taste terrible. That's because the oxygen has been mostly removed to keep its long shelf life stable. To make the water fresh and palatable, aerate it by pouring it from cup to cup. This will reconstitute the missing air making the water as fresh as ever.

Home Food:

20 lbs any type rice
2 bags of sugar
2 bags of flour
20 lbs of dried beans
2 large jars of peanut
6 bags of noodles
20 cans of fruit
20 cans of vegetables
20 cans of meat
Bouillon cubes
20 cans ready made sauce
Large box baking soda

Meat:

SPAM
Foiled packed tuna, chicken or salmon
Canned hams
pepperoni sticks, salted ham or bacon

This is a great time to use some of the recipes I suggested before. Play and experiment with them. It's fun, really. Get a case of PAM, also several small containers of Crisco or lard, which is pork fat and keeps without refrigeration even after being opened. At this point in your prepping you are just surviving -- not living in the lap of luxury.

Money and bartering

Over the years I've purchased items for my kit that looked good at
the time. Then after getting them home or using them I found they
just weren't for me. So I ended up giving them away or trashing
them. Now I keep a barter box; in this box are items we don't want
or use, but others certainly would have a use for . What's that
Grandpa used to say? "One man's poison is another man's tea." The
Vodka is to trade or make Molotov cocktails with.

My barter box:

Camp utensils
Camp food
Assorted knives
Warm hats
4 pints of vodka
Coffee packs
Various bullets
Canteens
Toothbrushes new
Aspirin
Fast food ketchup
Bic pens

Notebooks
Gun oil
Reading glasses
Tampons
Real soap, not camp
Diaper pins
Nail clippers
Fish hooks
Combs/brushes
Scissors small
Old paper matches
60% wool blanket
Assorted one-ounce bags of spices, salt, pepper, cayenne pepper, garlic, sugar, etc.

I would put some of these items in my BOB. In a SHTF event, spices will be precious, like gold. Imagine eating a squirrel or other critter without salt or pepper. Nah!

15th Poppa tip: Sugar and honey never go bad, another benefit is that they are naturally antiseptic for wounds.

Before 1964, quarters were made of 90% pure silver, and at this writing four 1964 quarters are worth nearly $20. Paper money may become useless, but I do keep about $40 in small bills just in case. Old silver coins or gold are easy to carry and don't take up much space or weight.

Find a like-minded friend or group

Many seasoned citizen Preppers already have a place where they can
bug out, which is one of the reasons for preparing a BOB.
Sometimes it's an old family farm or even just an empty plot of land.
Others have friends or family that already have rural property and
will take you in during times of unrest. For example, my wife and I
only have our home, although our home is ready for nearly any
disaster (except a direct hit from a tornado) that comes our way.
        We realized as I have mentioned before we just couldn't stay
in the home during times of civil unrest or WROL, as mentioned
before. When the masses that are dependent on city services run out
of food and fuels they will come looking for whatever they can get.
Hunger and fear will drive some normally good, kind Christian souls
into ravenous nervous hordes. A father or mother needing food for
their child will be as dangerous as a grizzly bear protecting its cubs.
Knowing my home's limitations and my ability to defend it from the
masses forced me to create a backup plan.

Fortunately, two of my like-minded dear friends that I have known for 30 years have large farms. One is a three-hour drive from my home, the other about an hour or so. I have planned to bug out and hike to the one I can get to the fastest. The down side to my friend's nearby property is that his farm will eventually come into the path of the lawless. The standard I was trained on is that massive gangs and other undesirables will have the resources to travel a minimum of 100 miles from the city in search of life-sustaining supplies. The downside to my other friend is the safe zone is more secure, but so far away. A decision of which friend to migrate toward we will make when the time comes. We are indeed prepared for both, as you must be as well.

16th Poppa tip: Vacant land is available at auctions or county land that has been repossessed can be purchased for mere dollars on the square foot.

How did I make and find these arrangements? Well, as I said I've been doing this for many years. Now the seasoned citizen needs to prepare for these safety zones by meeting like-minded people. Many of you will find individuals in your respective places of worship. Some will find groups on the Internet and there are many.

The requirements are that you bring what some call meat to the table, i.e., you must have something to offer a group for them to accept you. Are you a doctor, mechanic, carpenter, nurse or welder, perhaps a cook or a chef, a combat-trained soldier, police or fireman? Accountants and other what we used to call "pencil pushers" are important too, because they are organizers and they know how to easily assemble group inventories.

Any skill, any at all, is an important factor in being accepted. The point is before a group accepts you, you must bring something to the table.

Communication

The technology we enjoy today is wonderful, but if you boil away
the meat and get down to the bone, folks, all this new technology
involves really just basic communications; Notepads, iPhones, and
of course cellular phones with all their life confusing variations. I
remember some years back President Bush was flying into the
Charlotte airport for a visit to our fair city. I went to call home on my
cellular and to my dismay I found there wasn't a signal to be had.
When I got home I called the cellular company (on a landline)
thinking my phone was broken. I was advised that due to security
reasons all cellular activity was suspended while Air Force One
landed. I found out later that cellular phones can be activated to set
off a bomb, therefore with a push of a button the government could
effectively shut down the cellular towers.

      I also learned that these marvelous inventions were only as
good as the towers they could repeat from. Consequently, whenever
deep in the national forest, hunting, or just hiking, I often lost all
service without the ability to communicate with home or emergency
personnel. Of course, satellite phones are bulletproof; well, unless
the satellites fail. Besides, I don't have that kind of money to spend
on a phone.

To this day I have many friends and acquaintances that have given up their landlines in favor of the more "technology" advanced cellular phones and their new Voice Over Internet Phone. Or if they do maintain a landline it is often connected to a battery-operated phone. Big mistake my friends, as battery phones go out when the power to the base station goes out.

If you have a landline installed in your house, mobile home, apartment or cave there will be a box installed somewhere outside of the domicile where the phone line comes in. Often, even after a major power failure, there will still be power going to this phone, which generates independently from your local power company.

Plugging into this outside phone which already has a jack built in with (telling on my age) an old Princess-style phone or any phone that is not battery operated will give you the ability to communicate with the outside world for as long as the phone company supplies power to the line.

Establishing a meet location is critical. If a situation were to occur during the work week when most of the family is at work and the grandchildren are in school or at day care you should have a plan in place where everyone can meet at the beginning of a calamity. A backup location should also be put in place for meeting perhaps a week later after things calm down. The reason you'll want a backup is that it may take your family a few days to assemble.

For example, if the roads are clogged or electromagnetic pulses stops our electronics automobiles may also stop working. Make maps for these meeting or temporary safe zones and make sure everyone has one. You can also make generic maps (with symbols known only to family) as to where the bug-out-location is. According to the experts a large EMP burst from the sun only has a less than 15% chance of happening again. The last one was 1859. Hey! And the experts should know. Right? I mean it's not like they got a lousy track record or anything… Right?

17th Poppa tip: EMP are natural occurring phenomena caused by sunbursts or they can be man made from nuclear explosions. EMP fries electronic components and renders them useless. Old vehicles that do not have electronic ignitions, in theory, should not be affected. Of course, who the hell knows, with the exception of the military and some ancestors, nobody has ever experienced an EMP.

Also many tractors and airplanes that have Magneto motors will survive as well. To protect your electronics from EMP, consider building a "Faraday box" which shields the item from the EMP effects. Or buy a galvanized steel garbage can and store your BOB electronics in the sealed, rubber-lined can for a make shift Faraday box. A large, solid, insulated safe is a good location to store your hand-cranked radios along with any solar powering battery boxes you may have. The military began shielding their electronics or hard-casing them back in the 1980s.

Defense

Again, defense is a personal choice. Some of you are totally against having a firearm in the house. You need to have an alternative type of weapon you are comfortable with. In keeping with the Fear No Evil discipline, I would never be without some type of weapon in my home. Much of my thought process on this lifestyle comes from my military and law enforcement background, but you don't need this kind of background to learn about weapons.

Proficiency with a weapon of any type is a learned skill and Grandpa's adage about practice makes perfect rings true in the learning and use of any weapon, be it a knife, a stun gun, a firearm, or a bow and arrow. Guns are merely machines and like any machine you must practice with it until you are confident that you can use it safely and accurately. Gun classes are available in most towns or cities. Look into taking some classes and learn the proper techniques.

When my father was sixty years old I gave him a 1911, .45 caliber pistol for home defense. My dad was very comfortable with this weapon because he'd carried and used one during World War II from his landing on Normandy beach and all across Europe right into Germany. We would often go to the local range and practice whenever I could get down to his house in Florida. I realized when Dad hit his mid-seventies that he could no longer prepare the pistol to fire and was forgetting certain safety protocols one must implement to use the gun.

I felt he was no longer proficient with the firearm and I took it home with me. The look of despair in my Pop's eyes was more than I could stand. My hero was getting too old and frail to operate the machine. He needed a substitute to rebuild his confidence.

The easiest firearm to operate is a single-shot, 12-gauge shotgun. It's a simple machine. Basically open the barrel, place a shotgun shell in it, then close, cock the hammer and fire. Dad took solace in the fact that he could still defend his home if need be. He kept that weapon cleaned and oiled or "fit to fight," as he liked to say, until his passing at eighty.

I believe the best weapon a seasoned citizen could have on hand is a shotgun for home defense. I prefer the Mossberg pistol-grip model 500 shotgun. It's cheap, reliable, easy to use, holds six or more shells and you don't need a special permit to buy one.

As for a handgun, I would recommend a revolver, at least a .38 caliber. This is an excellent choice for a seasoned citizen purely for the weapon's simplicity and ease of operation. It has fewer moving parts than a pistol and is very easy to shoot. Smaller versions of the revolver are easy to carry concealed. (Requires a purchase permit and/or a concealed weapons permit to carry.)

Pistols, on the other hand, are wonderful firearms with many strong features. They can be powerful. The magazine capacity in some cases will hold eighteen rounds. That's a lot of bullets; however, the price one pays for these high capacity guns is that they require a bit more training along with maintenance. A pistol lacks the simplicity of a revolver for a seasoned citizen.

Dealing with illness and medicines

As seasoned citizens, many of us are taking prescription medicines just to stay alive and in the event of a catastrophic emergency these meds may not be available for some time. However with some preparation a person or family can be ready for an SHTF scenario and survive it. I always recommend that folks keep a minimum of three months supply of meds on hand, more if possible.

On your next doctor appointment explain how you feel about being prepared in the event of some type of disaster. But, what if your doctor refuses to help you prepare? Then find another doctor that has the same goals and objectives as your family. There are many out there. But remember, before taking or packing any medicines or alternative medicines, even herbs, make sure you check with a medical provider. Certain combinations of medicines and vitamins can be a deadly cocktail.

Your medicines will be more important now than ever before. For example, folks with diabetes will not be eating properly because emergency foods are not diabetes-friendly as they are designed to be packed with high carbohydrates for high-energy performance. With some shopping around or even on the Internet you will be able to find high protein foods that are available. Glycemic carbohydrates are what the nutritionists call good carbohydrates; they raise the sugar levels more slowly than regular carbohydrates. The fact of the matter is carbohydrates are a necessary part of life; one cannot live on protein alone.

"Rabbit fever" is an old condition our forefathers learned early on. They thought they would never starve because the rabbit and deer population was so abundant. They could just eat meat and live through the winter…WRONG. Without carbohydrates or fat, you will eventually die. Symptoms caused by lack of carbohydrates are tunnel vision, then blurred vision and eventually death. Consider wheat-flour pasta, steel-cut oats or brown rice. Again, if you don't have a computer or are not computer literate take someone with Internet experience to the local library and do your research while you can.

The new insulin pens can be kept much longer than regular insulin without refrigeration and there are coolers that will run off batteries to keep regular insulin cool. You can also use solar power to re-charge the unit and some can recharge off your car battery.

Study home remedies; there are numerous books on the subject. Learn about herbs that are helpful to your particular medical problem in your particular part of the world. Veterinarians are an excellent source of medicines if you can find a like-minded doctor.

Stock up on healthy liquids that have a long shelf life. Ensure is an excellent choice for seasoned citizens that need to keep up with their fiber and vitamins.

Recreational canned oxygen is widely available without prescription and may help those of us with breathing disorders in lieu of inhalers that can no longer be purchased. It's not a perfect solution, but it may help until order is restored.

Consider a small propane generator that will keep life-sustaining machines running through times of crisis. Gasoline generators are noisy and gasoline spoils, turning into vanish after a few months. Inhibitors only last a few more months and propane canisters are prevalent. They are storable and they won't go bad when you need them. Ask your local electrician what size generator you will need to keep the life-giving machines operating.

Check on buying an electrical inverter that converts you vehicle's direct-current battery DC power to alternating AC power, allowing you to run the machines more efficiently even with the engine off. This technique works whether at home or in the field. Northern Hydraulics carries a reasonably priced solar panel that will charge your car batteries even during cloudy weather. The inverter will power many small machines.

Budget constraints

Preparing your family and home for unforeseen dangers is basically just insurance. Most of us pay for some type of insurance in our daily lives. Self-reliance does not have to cost a small fortune. In fact, you can begin even on a fixed income.

Starting the next time you go to the store for groceries, just buy one extra can of food. Do this each time you buy groceries and in a few short months you'll start to notice your long-term food storage growing.

Canned hams
Tuna fish
Corn beef hash
Peanut butter
SPAM
Hormel ready eat meals
Beans/oatmeal
Canned chicken
Sardines
Soups, canned and powdered

Remember the expiration date does not mean the food has gone bad. It's just the manufacturer's suggested use-by date. Buying these long-term food items is so much cheaper than buying packaged camping food. One boneless canned ham easily feeds a family of four.

Save your soda bottles such as the one-liter large bottle. Soda bottles are food-grade plastic. They won't leach any nasty chemicals into the food stored in the bottle. Take a one-liter soda bottle and using a funnel, fill the bottle with you favorite dry food. Beans, rice, or noodles, etc. Soda bottles are under pressure so their caps are stronger than a water bottle, and are therefore better to store food in.

Place an oxygen absorber in the bottle and seal it tight. If space is an issue in your home, then store the filled bottles under the beds or behind the couches out of sight. Never in the hot attic, as the strong, dry heat rapidly deteriorates the food.

Oxygen absorbers can be purchased in many food stores or online. Remember the absorbers have a shelf life as well and the clock will start ticking as soon as you open the bag. When the bag's color changes from green to blue or blue to green it means the absorber is in its final days of working. Once sealed in the bottle they will last for years.

Many foods today come pre-packed with oxygen absorbers which are basically composed of a fungus that inhibits oxygen, thereby allowing to food to last longer. We reuse these absorbers in our packed food as long as the seals are intact.

Water purification

We must have pure clean water to drink, wash and cook with daily.
We can only survive three days without consuming this life-giving
fluid. One way water can be cleaned is by chemical means. Iodine
tablets were the standard, and although they make the water taste
terrible, they are still widely available. The bad taste can be abated
by mixing a sports-drink powder or you can buy a tablet (which is
just vitamin C) that removes the bad taste. Because these tabs are so
plentiful they are the mainstay in my water-purifying arsenal, as two
tabs will clean a quart or liter of water in little more than 30 minutes.
The tab bottles are very small, thereby allowing us to carry several
months' supply without effort.

    Chlorine dioxide tabs are my next choice for cleaning water
chemically. It is recommended you let the single tab rest in the water
for a total of four hours to allow it to absolutely cleanse the fluid.
The gas removes giardia, cryptosporidium, bacteria, viruses and
cysts. The best part is after four hours, then opening the cap for ten
minutes to let the gas escape, you'll have the best-tasting, clean,
crisp water ever, so much better than bottled water. I really enjoy
this purifier, however it is pricey as 12 tabs will clean three gallons.

    Boiling is always safe. Actually, just getting the water up to
about 180-190 degrees will kill any bad stuff. I normally take it right
to just boiling then remove the water from the heat.

Third-world countries use ultra-violet light; they strain water into clear plastic bottles then cap and set the bottles on a tin roof or slab of metal. The water will sit like that all day in direct sunlight, the penetrating ultra-violet rays killing all bacteria. The bottles cool during the night and are ready to drink the next morning.

A similar method that is becoming very popular is a SteriPEN, which is an ultraviolet light about the size of a small pen. They say it will purify one liter of water in 90 seconds by simply stirring the water in the bottle; when the red light turns green the water is clean. Ultra-violet lights are installed on some wells where the water is deemed less than palatable. Using ultra-violet is a natural way to cleanse water; exactly like the Sun only these SteriPEN devices do it much faster.

As I said earlier, my pack is simple and void of most high-tech items, but if you're a gadget person there are plenty out there. Remember, water purifying will not remove chemicals with the exception of some silver removing products, so keep this in mind when gathering from questionable water sources near nuclear-power plant dams, and of course, industrial areas.

The various purifiers mentioned here are enough for you to get started and experiment with at home before applying them to the field. Water purifying is a learned skill that requires more information than I can supply. Purifiers run the gamut from mundane water straws to sophisticated countertop units.

Conclusion

This guide is enough to get you on track and also thinking about being prepared. I have addressed how to research the sections outlined at a library or on the Internet. There are trusted sources for finding then purchasing the equipment you will need in a bug-in or bug-out scenario. The sources I listed are my sources for food and equipment, including vendors, that I have had a long, buying relationship with over the years.

This book is meant to get you on the road to self-reliance and it's a road you should enjoy traveling. Hopefully, we will never need to bring into play what was learned on these pages; however, if we do then we can take solace in the fact that our equipment, along with our knowledge, will pull us through nearly any situation quite comfortably.

Stay prepared, live free, and Fear No Evil
Poppa John